Who's Six?

Gordon Winch & Gregory Blaxell
Illustrated by Joe Spellman

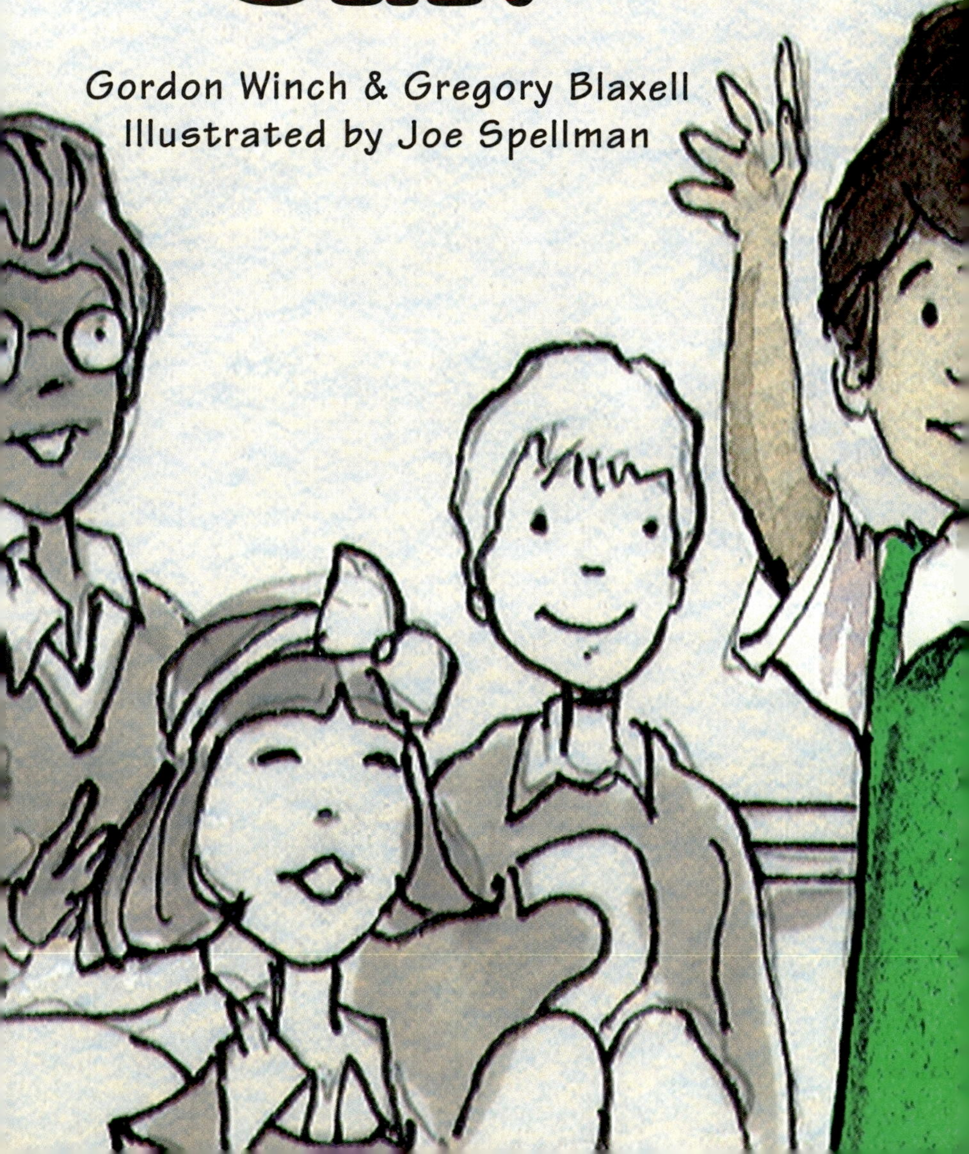

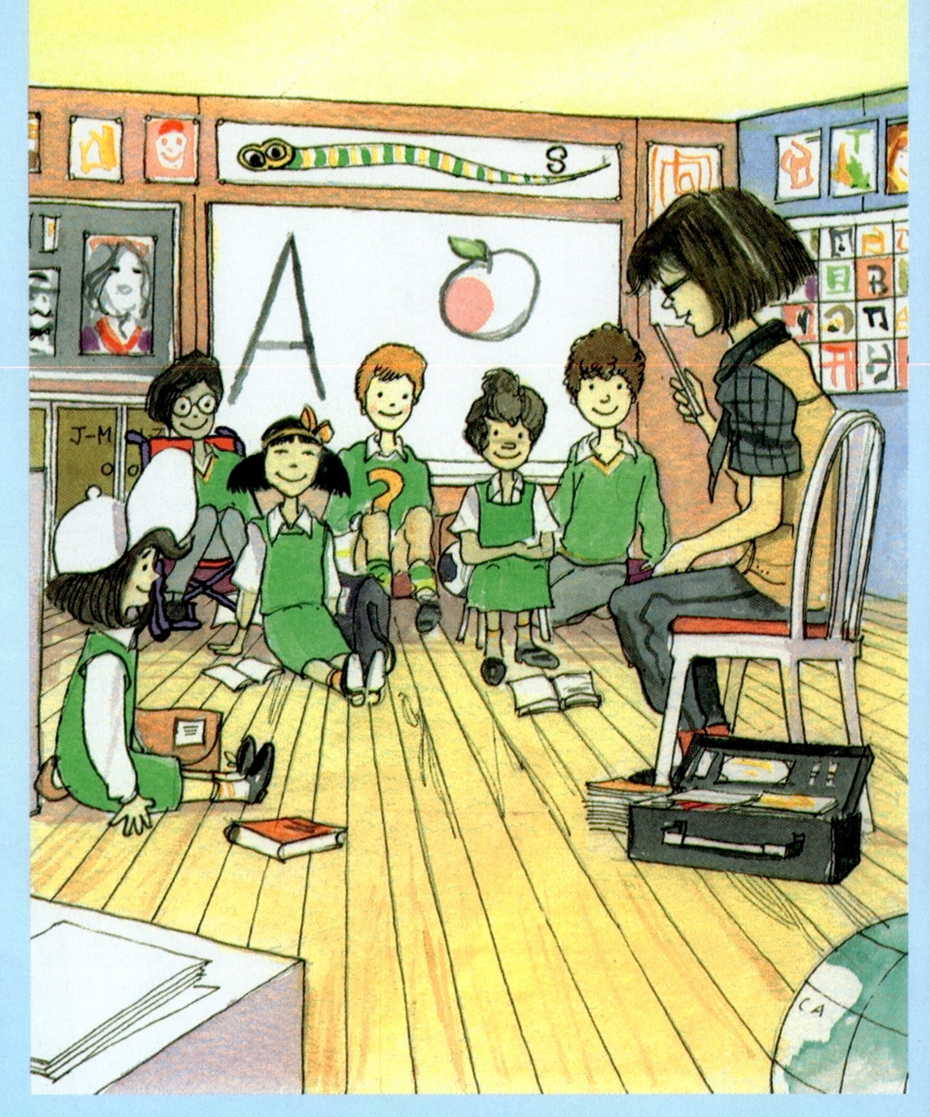

Who's six?

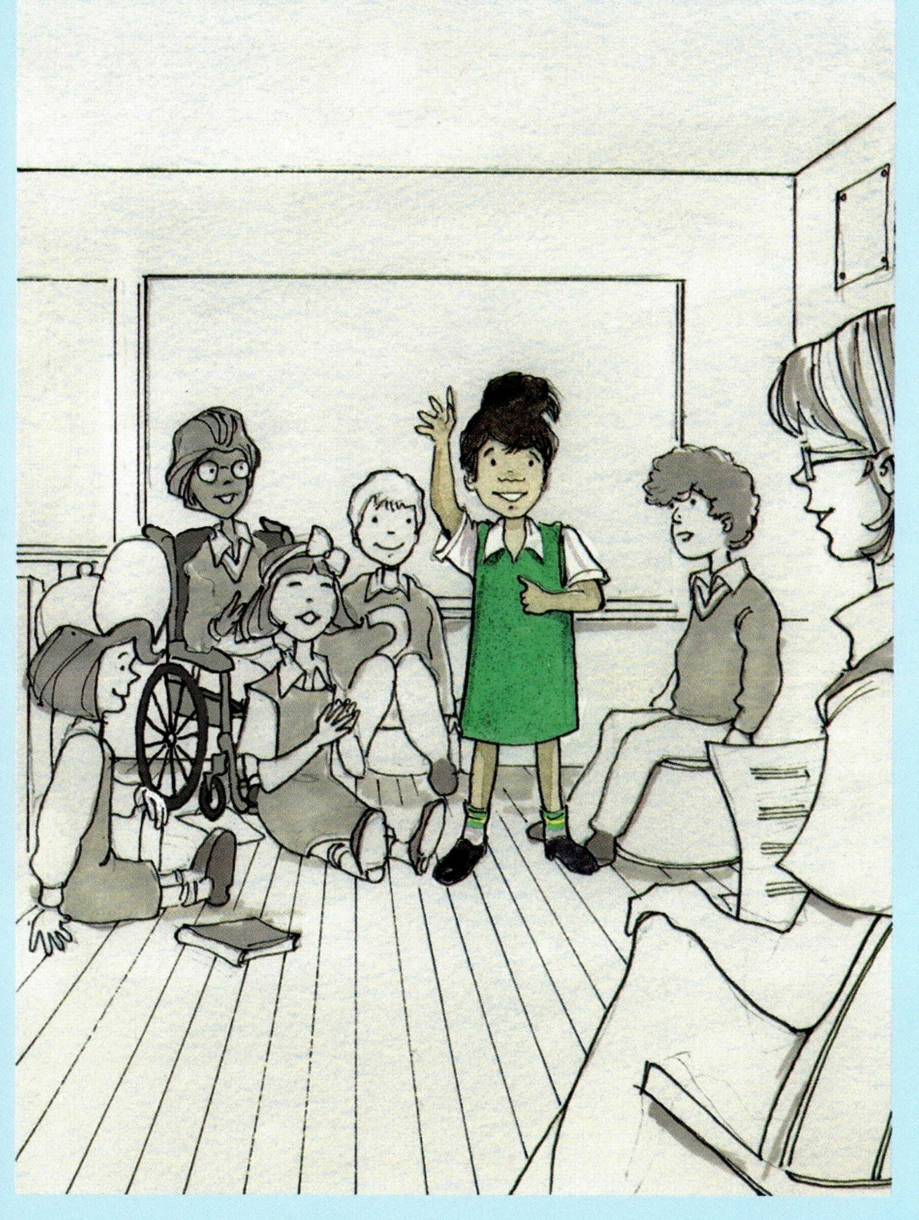

I am.

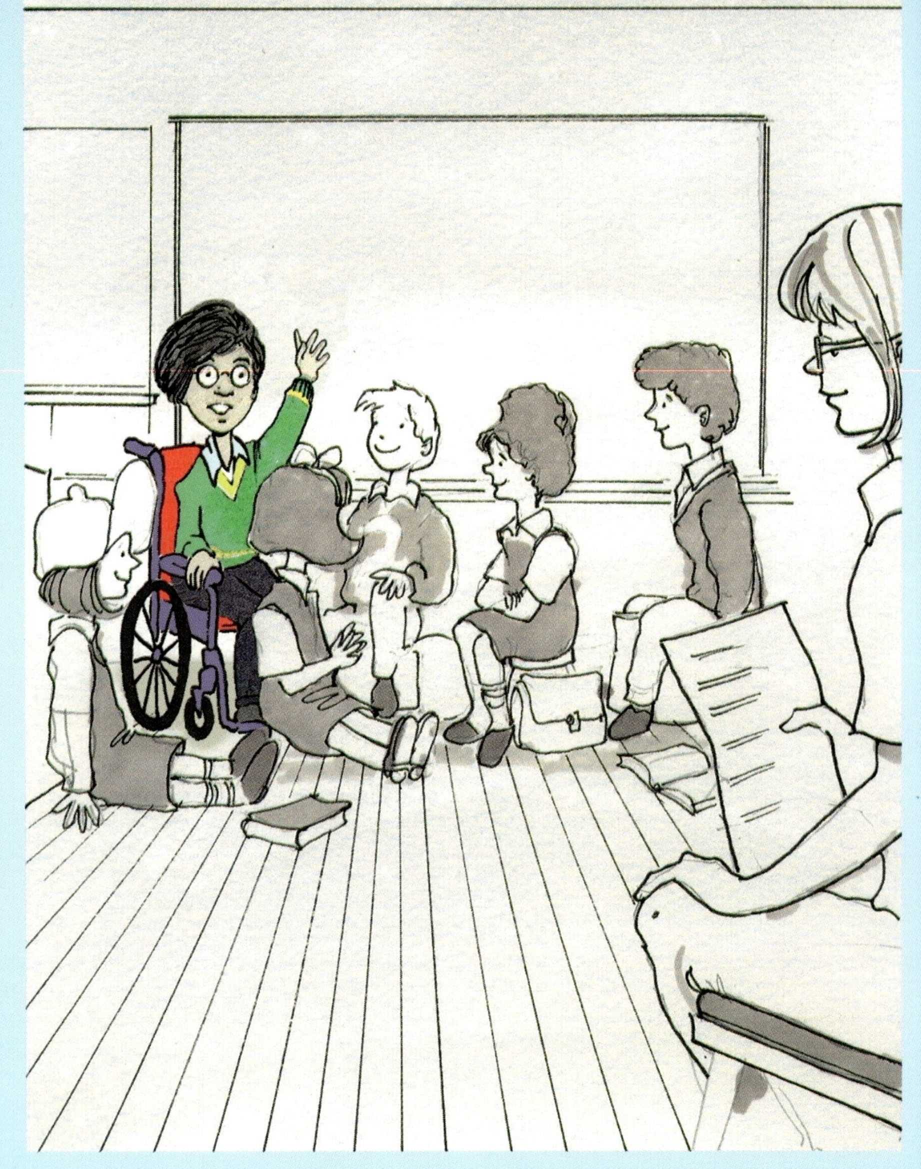

I am.

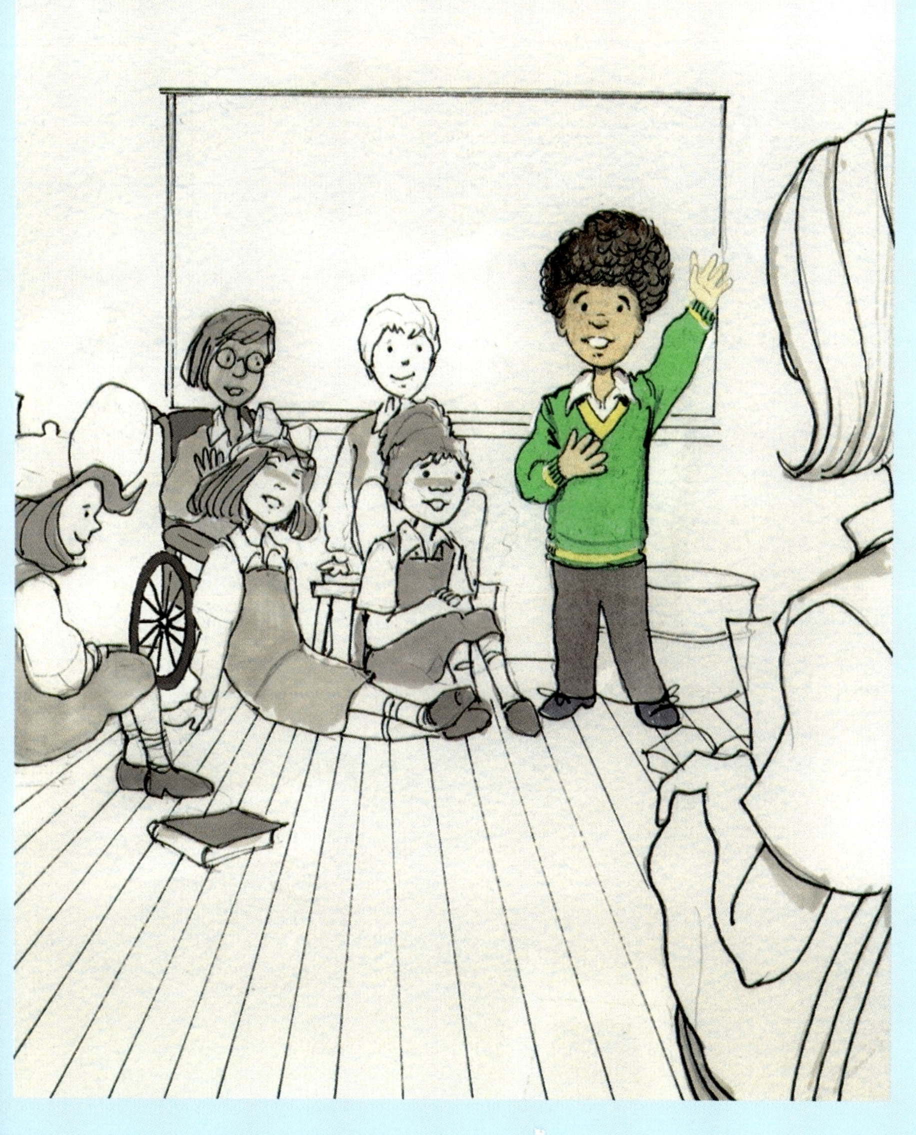

I am.

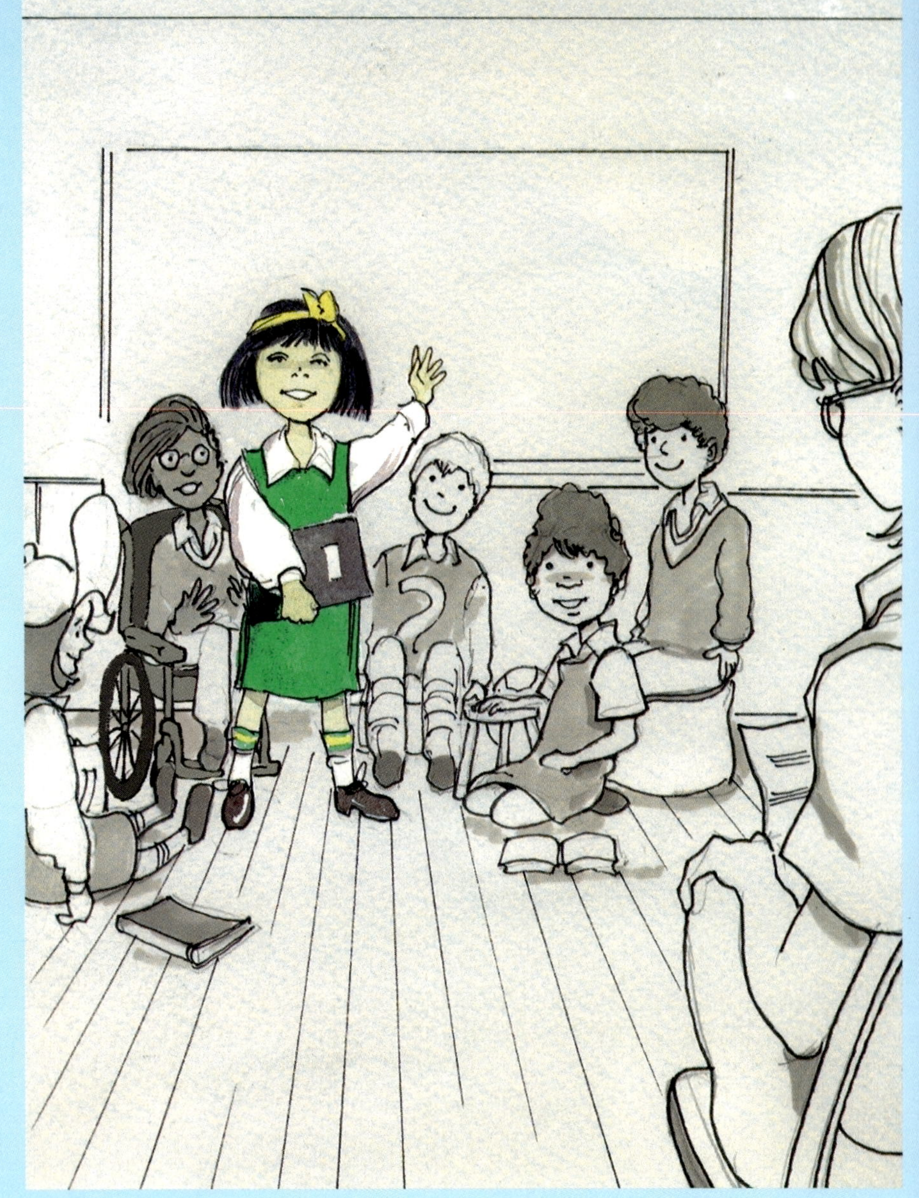

I am.

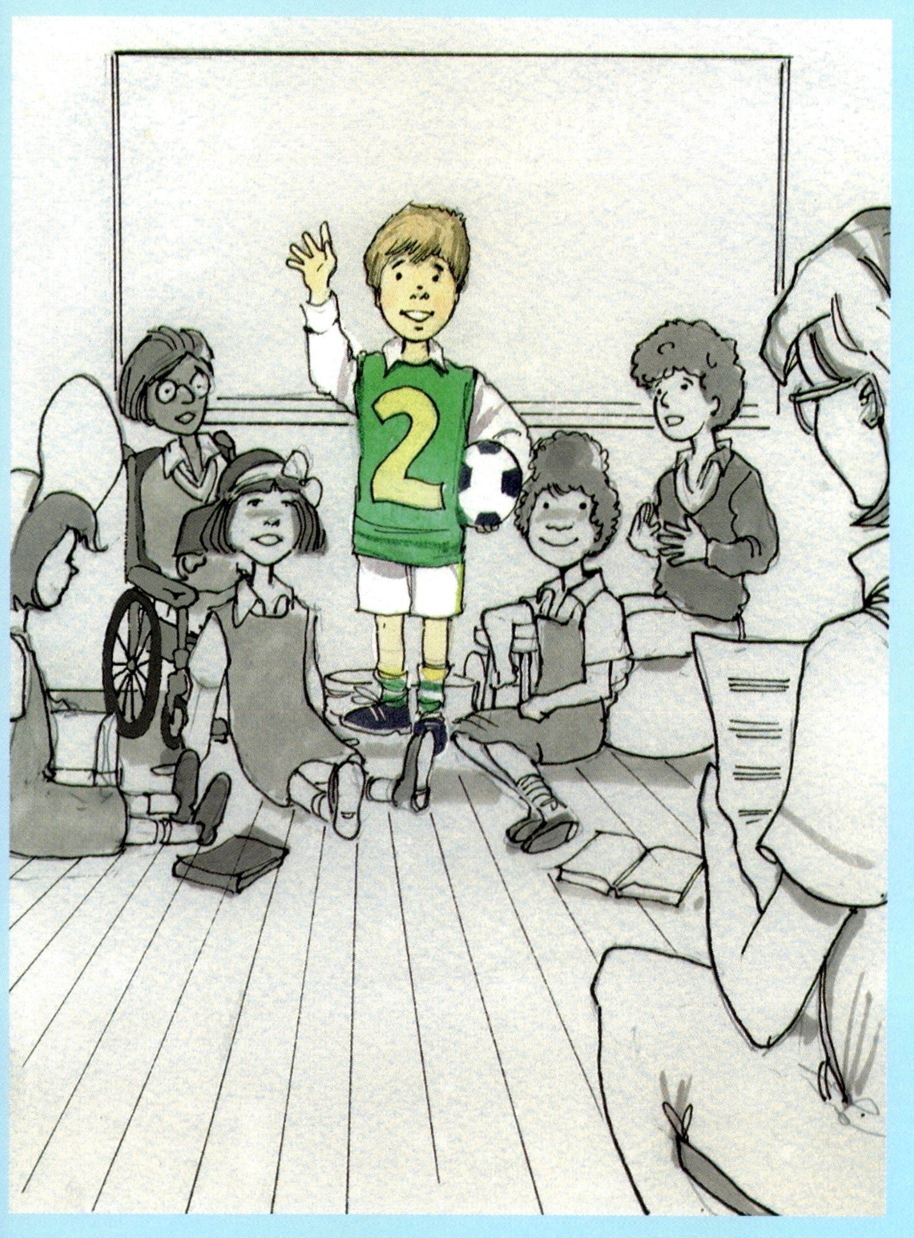

I am.

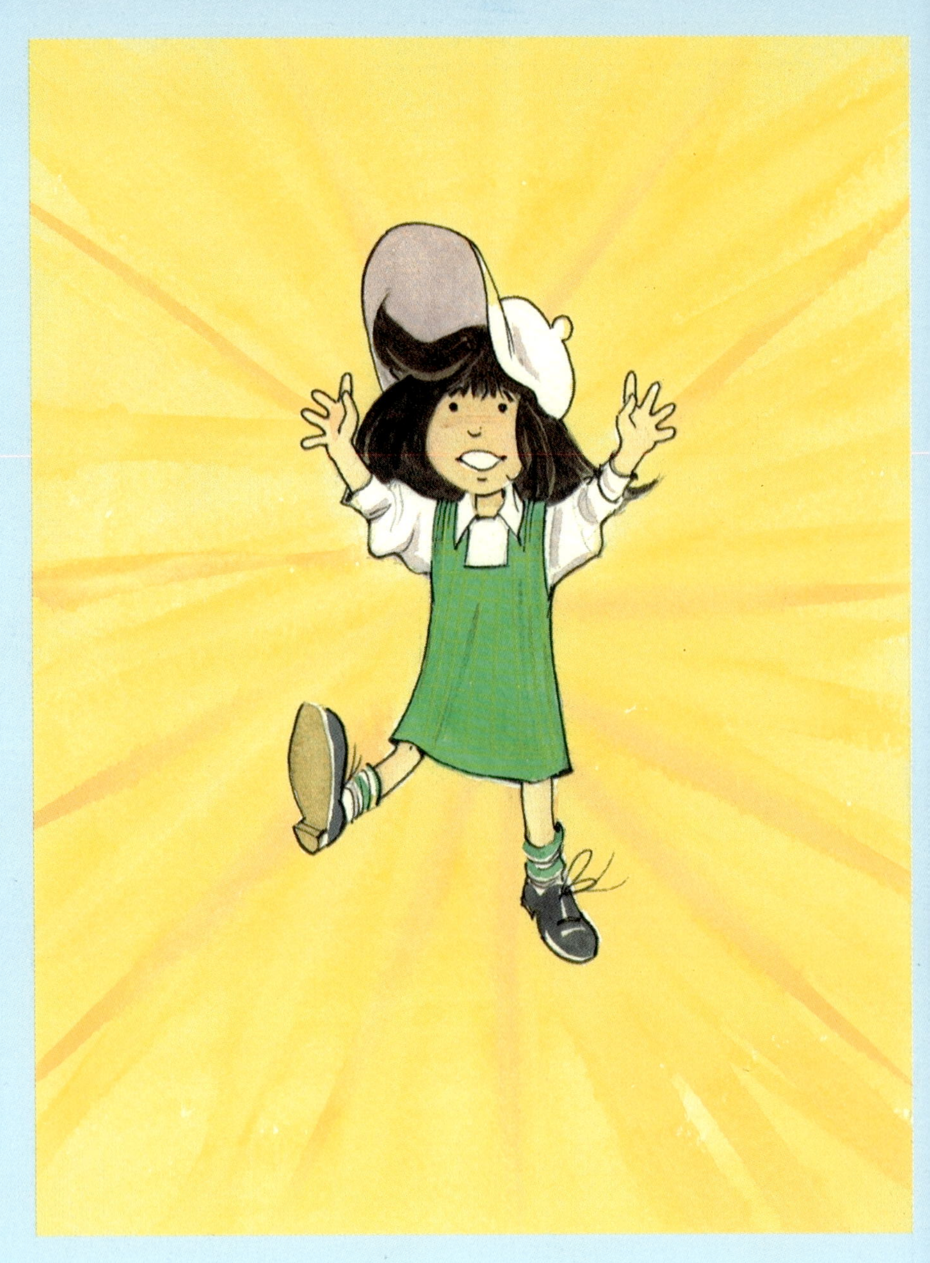

I'm five and a half.